SAND ART

*materials
techniques
terrariums
sandpainting
sculpture
projects*

Ellen Appel

CROWN PUBLISHERS, INC., NEW YORK

Dedicated to Joel,
first of all; Sid and Sue for their wonderful enthusiasm
and encouragement; and Janis

Inquiries should be addressed to Crown Publishers, Inc., One Park Avenue,
New York, N.Y. 10016

Printed in the United States of America
Published simultaneously in Canada by
General Publishing Company Limited

Designed by Shari de Miskey

Library of Congress Cataloging in Publication Data

Appel, Ellen.
    Sand art.

    Includes index.
    1. Sand craft.   I.   Title.
TT865.A66 1976   745.5   75-42215
ISBN 0-517-52475-9
ISBN 0-517-52476-4 pbk.

Note: All photographs, unless otherwise credited,
are by Joel Fried and the author.

Contents

1 SAND ART: AN EXCITING NEW CRAFT   1

2 THE BASICS   3

Materials   3
Design Tools   3
Choosing a Container   4
Sand   7
Optional Materials   8
Making Sand Designs   8
Pictures   12
Choosing a Picture   13
Some Problems: A Mistake   15
What to Do with Waste Sand   16
Sticking Sand   16
Sealing the Sand Design   17
Caring for Sand Art Objects   18

3 CACTUS POTS, TERRARIUMS, AND OTHER PLANTERS   19

Cactus Pots and a Scallop Design   19
Terrariums and a Landscape Design   29
Caring for Sand Art Terrariums   34
Bottle Terrariums   36
Other Planters   37
Caring for Sand Art Planters   41

4 FLORAL SETTINGS   43

Vases and a Geometric Design   43
Flowers under Glass and a Floral Design   49
The Floral Centerpiece   55

5 SANDPAINTINGS   57

Indian Sandpainting: The Permanent Technique   58
General Sandpainting Rules   60
Traditional Sandpainting   62
Contemporary Sandpainting   64
Sandpainted Objects   68
Three-Dimensional Sandpaintings and a Seascape Design   69
Glass and Wood Framed Paintings   76

6 SAND ART SCULPTURES   78

The Decorative Cylinder   78
Words, Letters, and a ''L-O-V-E'' Design   80
Turning the Boxes Upside Down   83
Representational Forms   84
The Face and Making Facial Features   84
Display Cases and a Mushroom Design   89

7 SAND-AROUND-THE-HOUSE   93

The Fishbowl and a Shell Design   93
Utensil Holders and a Train Design   97
Lamps   102
Candle Holders   104
Serving Pieces   107
The Terrarium Table and Constructing a Cube   107
A Checkerboard Table and Filling a Tabletop with Sand Art   109

SUPPLY SOURCES   113

INDEX   115

Some sand art projects are flowers under glass, a decorative cylinder, multilevel cactus planter, vase, and utensil holder.

1 Sand Art: An Exciting New Craft

Up until recently only children building sandcastles on the beach ever thought of sand as an art medium. But now a beautiful new use has been found for sand, and sand art has become today's most exciting new form of creative expression.

Although forms of sandpainting have existed for centuries in American Indian religious custom, the modern version is totally unique. In modern sand art sand patterns or pictures are formed inside glass or plastic containers. These designs are built up with different colors of sand, and then poked or pushed into shape with paintbrushes, spoons, and pointed tools.

The reasons for the popularity of sand art are obvious to all who have tried the craft. It is unique, inexpensive, and surprisingly easy to do. Project possibilities are nearly unilimited. Sand art works well in planters, terrariums, vases, lamps, tables, sculptures, and many more practical or purely decorative items.

This book explores these and other sand art projects. It also gives step-by-step instructions for many different sand art designs, including a landscape, seascape, face, flower, and sample abstract patterns. Special artistic talent is not required for any design or project. All that is needed is a knowledge of the basic techniques, some practice, and imagination.

A list of materials and an explanation of the basic sand art techniques are given in the following chapter. It is important to understand this basic information before attempting any of the sand art designs. The information applies to every design in the book as well as original designs of your own.

The book is organized into project categories, and designs are presented in the context of particular projects. Similar sand art designs can be made in any size or shape container. In fact, many demonstrated designs are repeated in other sand art projects throughout the book.

For the beginner it is best to follow the designs as shown. Even if you follow the instructions exactly, choice of color and your own distinctive touch will distinguish your sand art object from all others. Exact duplications are not possible in sand art. It is a gentle craft, with no perfect forms. Patterns will always be somewhat irregular, and pictures less than realistic. This is one of the charms of the craft. No matter how carefully you copy a design, the result is yours alone.

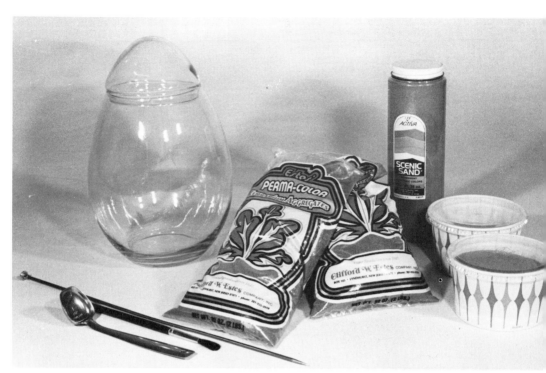

Materials for sand art are a clear container; common household utensils including spoon, paintbrush, and pointed tool; and several colors of sand. Shown are three different brands of colored sand.

Sand design tools are common household utensils such as a knitting needle, swizzle stick, skewer, broken plastic fork, wooden stylus, or other pointed tool; a spoon bent into a ladle shape, paintbrush, and flat coffee stirring stick.

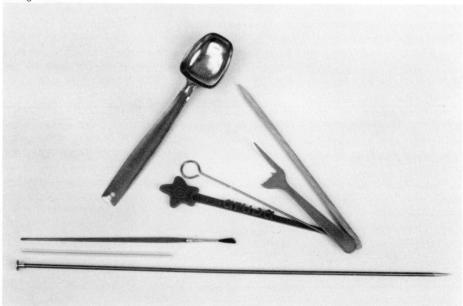

2
The Basics

MATERIALS

All you need for sand art is a clear container, a few common tools, and several colors of sand. Materials are inexpensive, and most are probably already in your home. Ordinary household utensils are perfect designing tools, and any clear jar can be used as a sand art container. Of all the necessary supplies colored sand is the only item most people are without. But because of the popularity of sand art, colored sand is now easy to find.

DESIGN TOOLS

For most designs the only necessary tools are a paintbrush, pointed tool, and spoon. For special effects or containers with unusual shapes other utensils are occasionally called for. But even these are easy enough to find in most homes.

An ordinary knitting needle makes a perfect pointed tool. If you prefer, you can substitute a skewer, pointed swizzle stick, wooden stylus, or broken plastic fork. The pointed tool fills most designing requirements. But sometimes you may need other tools. For example, you may need a flat squared-off tool for special geometric designs or a curved tool for small-mouthed or extremely skinny containers. The squared-off tool can be a flat coffee stirrer and the curved tool can simply be a knitting needle bent by pliers.

It doesn't really matter which design tools you use. If it works, it is a good sand art tool. And to work it must reach all parts of the container, all the way down to the bottom and into all corners. In a wide straight-sided container one tool taller than the container is probably all you will need. In unusual-shaped containers one tool may not fit all the requirements. Determine what you need for each individual project, and use as many design tools as necessary.

A paintbrush is also needed in sand art. It is used to smooth sand, shape designs, and brush unwanted sand from the sides of the container. Any paintbrush will do. Like the design tool, it simply must be taller than the container and be able to reach everywhere inside.

A spoon is the last important sand art tool. It lets you place sand exactly where you want it. Ordinary spoons are fine, and long iced-tea spoons are even better. Probably the best spoons are inexpensive metal measuring spoons. They are usually thin and can easily be bent into a ladle shape. This way sand can be carried efficiently into the container on just the right size spoon for each design section.

With the proper container any project is possible. Here flexible plastic tubing was filled with sand for these modern necklaces. *Photo, Susan Lessner Goodrich*

CHOOSING A CONTAINER

The possibilities for sand art projects are as vast as the types of containers available to fill with sand art designs. As long as you have the proper container, almost anything can be made with sand art—from tiny planters to substantial tables. You can use bottles and jars that might otherwise be thrown away, purchase special containers, or construct your own.

Empty wine bottles are prime candidates for sand art containers. So are many other throwaways such as old fishbowls, glasses, and cruets that come free with dry salad dressing. Cylinders, apothecary jars, glass eggs, and plastic cubes are inexpensive and easy to find in housewares departments and variety stores. Chemical supply labs also sell wonderful sand art containers, including all shapes of glass flasks and test tubes to insert in sand art vases. Another good container source is the flea market. What a non-sand artist offers for 50¢ may be inspiration for a spectacular sand art object. Look around for the best shape for your project, or let the container itself inspire a sand art idea.

Clear containers naturally display colors best. But do not automatically discard tinted jars. Wine bottles, with their greenish cast, tend to soften the colors of the sand within. As long as the tint is light, the results can be extremely interesting.

Both glass and plastic containers work well with sand art. Take special care with plastics, however, because they scratch easily. Also, since sand has a tendency to stick to plastic, be sure to wipe the entire container with an anti-static preparation before beginning the sand art design. Always use a soft cloth so that no scratches occur during this process. Anti-static cloths or sprays are available at most record shops.

Prolific sand artists often use plastics because it is relatively simple to construct containers in the perfect shape for each particular project. Directions are given on page 107 for constructing a plastic terrarium table. These basic instructions can be applied to any plastic cube or rectangle.

Empty wine bottles, cylinder storage jars, and plastic boxes are good sand art containers.

To prevent sand from sticking to plastic containers, use an anti-static preparation before beginning sand designs.

Many containers are specifically made for the purpose you have in mind. These containers, for example, are from a line of terrarium jars made by the Riekes-Crisa Company.

Some of the best sand art containers are found in unlikely places. These containers come from a pet shop, a chemistry supply lab, and the salad dressing department of a supermarket.

Container size determines the total amount of sand needed. The 3″ x 2¼″ x 2¼″ plastic box requires 12 ounces sand; the 7¼″ cylinder with 3½″ diameter uses 3½ pounds; and the tapering 7½″ cruet needs only 18 ounces.

SAND

Largely due to the current popularity of sand art, colored sand is now available at many different sources. Today, garden centers, florists, variety stores, and aquarium shops are all likely to carry sand in an assortment of colors, and in several brands. And like other products, there are differences between each brand. Price, grain size, and intensity of color all vary. It is important to consider all these qualities when choosing sand for your projects. In addition, if the project is a fishbowl or planter, be sure sand is nontoxic and colorfast. In fact, any project that has the potential of getting wet, including vases, should be made with colorfast sand.

The amount of sand needed depends upon the size of your container. This is something that becomes easier to judge after a few sand art projects. Do not necessarily eliminate large containers because of the huge amount of sand they will need. Since a sand design is only on the outside anyway, the center of the container can be fllled with potting soil for plant projects, waste sand, or beach sand.

You will need at least two colors of sand for any design. Most projects in this book use four to seven colors. Choose colors to harmonize with your decorating scheme or match flowers, plants, or other elements to be displayed in the finished object. You may prefer vibrant colors, earthy tones, or pale pastels. Use realistic colors or improve upon mother nature. In any sand art design just let your color sense guide you.

Grain size is an important factor in choosing sand. This often varies substantially in the case of different brands. Fine-grained and coarse-grained sands have their own advantages, and you may wish to experiment with both types. Fine-grained sand is especially good for pictures and delicate abstracts. It makes detail work easier, and the outlines between colors seem "cleaner."

On the other hand, the rough distinctive texture of a sand design is far more obvious with coarse grains. So before you opt for fine-grained sand, remember it is this quality, after all, that gives sand art its gentle, irregular look and distinguishes the craft from any other medium.

OPTIONAL MATERIALS

Besides all the basics described in the last few pages, you may find a few other materials helpful. First, it is a good idea to cover the work area with lots of newspaper. Clear plastic cups are also handy for each color of sand. In addition, you may prefer to work on a turntable or lazy susan. This way the container can be turned as you work and viewed from all angles.

Nothing else is needed for most sand art designs. Individual projects, such as planters or floral displays, naturally require other supplies such as plants or dried flowers. All special supplies are listed for projects demonstrated in this book. This includes everything unique to that project, plus a suggestion for the container shape and some of the sand colors.

Now that you know what materials you need, gather the basic supplies and try out the design techniques described on pages 8–15.

MAKING SAND DESIGNS

In subsequent chapters sample sand patterns and pictures are illustrated in step-by-step photographs. All these designs plus any you create on your own follow the basic principles outlined here.

STRAIGHT LAYERING

To start a simple layered pattern pour one color of sand into the container and smooth top edges straight and level with a paintbrush. If sand sticks to the sides, brush it down before pouring the next layer.

By smoothing all layers straight and level, your design will look something like this.

CONTOURED LAYERS

Instead of smoothing layers, you can contour top edges with a spoon or paintbrush.

By contouring all layers that follow, your design will look similar to this.

By pouring layers and making design points with a knitting needle or other pointed tool you can create fascinating sand patterns. The design point is the basis for all abstracts. It is needed for the sample scalloped design and geometric pattern demonstrated in later chapters, and for most patterns you will create on your own.

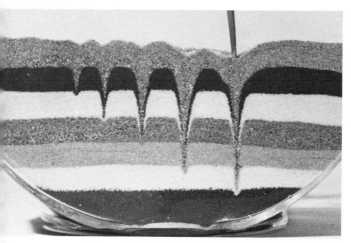

MAKING DESIGN POINTS

Design points may plunge through any number of layers. They are made by poking into the sand after two or more layers have been poured.

To make a design point slowly push your pointed tool down into the sand while holding the point firmly against the container. This will cause the lower layer to be displaced, and sand from the upper layer will flow in. This way a design point is created.

Pull the tool toward the center of the container before lifting it out of the sand. The tool should be about ½" from the side when it is removed.

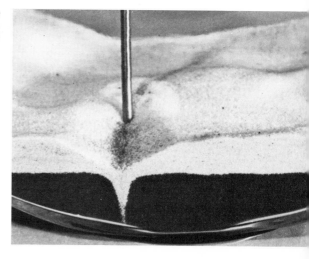

Make wider design points with a wider tool. Or widen design points by poking more than once with your regular tool.

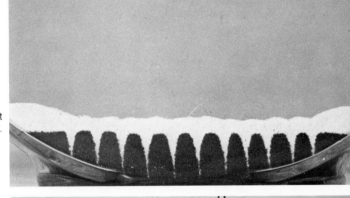

TURNING DESIGN POINTS INTO PATTERNS

Most patterns start with design points at regular intervals all around the container.

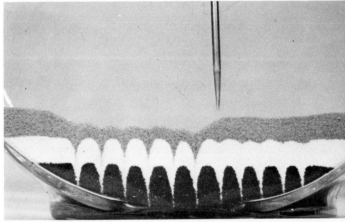

When the next layer is poured, a simple pattern can be made by creating new design points directly above the original design points.

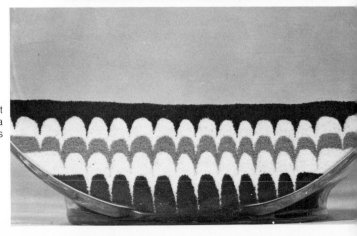

When design points in all subsequent layers follow the original design points, a pattern similar to this one will result. This is a simple scalloped design.

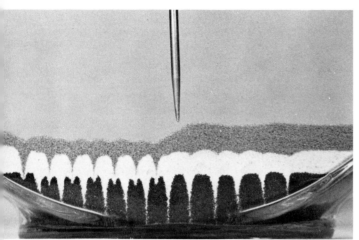

Another simple design approach is to poke between the original design points.

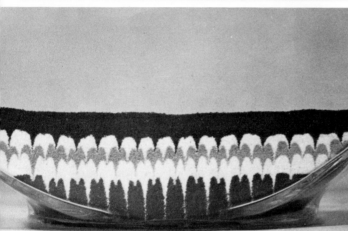

When design points in all subsequent layers are made between design points in the layer beneath, a pattern something like this one will result.

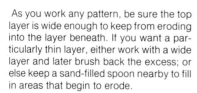

As you work any pattern, be sure the top layer is wide enough to keep from eroding into the layer beneath. If you want a particularly thin layer, either work with a wide layer and later brush back the excess; or else keep a sand-filled spoon nearby to fill in areas that begin to erode.

PICTURES

Once the basic design techniques are mastered, it is easy to create pictures in sand. First read the principles described for making sand designs and the additional picture-making techniques on the next few pages. Together they include all the fundamentals for making landscapes, seascapes, faces, and any pictures, no matter how large or complex-looking.

CHOOSING A PICTURE

Deciding upon a picture can be as challenging as learning to make it. Not every artist, sand art or otherwise, can paint from imagination. For the beginner it is helpful to start with a picture described in this book. Later, elements of different pictures can be combined into original sand designs. For totally different designs it is a good idea to make a rough sketch first or work from a photograph. The sand art clouds pictured here were copied from a portion of a painting. Using basic picture-making techniques, small scenic sections or whole panoramas can be translated into sand art.

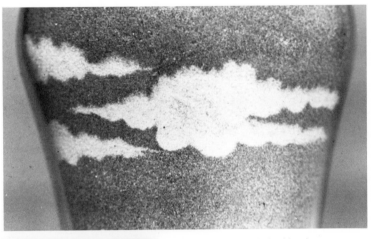

The sand art clouds in this glass were faithfully copied from the sky section of the art print at left.

PICTURE MAKING

For all pictures use a spoon bent into a ladle shape to place sand where desired. Since the picture appears on the outside only, place the sand against the side of the container. Here a simple mountain is made with a mound of sand.

Smooth or contour the top edges. Or, if you are satisfied with the shape as it was poured, leave it alone and go on to the next step.

Build pictures up evenly all around the container in small sections at a time. Be sure to keep the center of the container filled as well. The sand in the center will not show, so this is a good place for waste sand or other filler materials.

Cover shapes with sand in a contrasting color. Start pouring sand into the low areas, filling in the area around and in back of the shapes. Eventually, build up to the higher areas, finally covering the shapes. Pour slowly and always from behind the shapes. This prevents the shapes from flattening under the weight of the new sand. Never pour from above.

To steepen diagonal lines, as in sailboats or steep mountain peaks, run a pointed tool along the top edge of the covered shape.

To straighten the sides of shapes, as in mushroom stems, squares, or even circle sides, insert a tool ¼" to ½" from the shape and gently push toward it. The pressure of the outside sand will flatten the shape and make the side somewhat vertical. Straighten large shapes a small amount at a time by withdrawing the tool and repeating the step.

SOME PROBLEMS: A MISTAKE

Everyone makes mistakes, even in sand art. But do not consider your sand design a total loss just because you do not like a color combination, or a shape is not turning out right. Generally, small mistakes will not even be noticed. But if you feel something should be changed, the unwanted sand can simply be scooped out and the area redone.

FIXING A MISTAKE

If your sun will not round out, or if you are unhappy with any part of a design, scoop out the affected area with a spoon.

Remove the entire unwanted shape plus all the sand above it.

Brush back all remaining grains of unwanted colors. Then start over again.

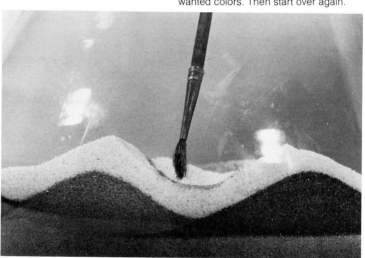

WHAT TO DO WITH WASTE SAND

Waste sand can either be hidden in the center of a container or incorporated into the design. When waste sand is mixed throughly, it can be used as a distinct new color. The salt and pepper look of mixed colors contrasts well with pure shades.

STICKING SAND

Sand sticking to the sides as it is poured into the container will make designs appear fuzzy. A few precautions can prevent this problem. First, use an anti-static preparation on all plastic containers as described on page 5. Then be sure your container,

The salt and pepper mountain in the center of the design is made of waste sand.

whether glass or plastic, is absolutely dry. The sand as well must be dry before any project is begun. Where moisture or static is not present, any stray sand on the container sides can easily be brushed down with a paintbrush.

SEALING THE SAND DESIGN

In certain projects it is necessary to seal in the sand design, whether to protect an especially vulnerable top layer or to allow the entire container to be turned upside down. Different methods of sealing these particular sand art objects are described in later chapters. Each is presented in the context of the project to which it applies.

If desired, any sand design may be sealed to prevent accidental shifting. An effective way of sealing sand in all types of projects is with a preparation like Terraseal, available at Agroth, Inc. in New York City. (Check the Supply Source section for the full address.) This type of sealer, made especially for sand designs, does not alter the appearance of the design. And unlike most other methods, it leaves practically no trace. It is simply mixed with water and slowly poured over the finished sand art design. When the sand dries, the design is solid.

The Terraseal method may be used for vases, planters, three-dimensional sandpaintings, or any other sand art object. It may also be substituted for any other sealing method described in this book. This particular preparation works with most brands of sand, especially coarser grained sands. However, before pouring it into your design, test with leftover sand from the same project. In addition, if you plan to use it in a plastic container, make sure all seams are watertight before beginning your sand design.

CARING FOR SAND ART OBJECTS

A sand design, like any other work of art, requires special care. Since it is composed of loose grains of sand, objects must be kept upright at all times. Do not turn the container over or shake it up. With rough handling, the sand will shift.

Use both hands to move large objects. They are often heavier than they look. To keep the weight distributed evenly, carry all containers, even relatively small ones, with your hands on the bottom.

Sand art objects, whether sealed or in a natural, loose state, will last indefinitely with a reasonable amount of care. Proper handling and careful treatment will allow every one of your sand art objects to remain beautiful for many years to come.

3
Cactus Pots, Terrariums, and Other Planters

It is no wonder that sand art first became popular when it was combined with plants. Today green plants fill corners and windows of almost every home. And as a decorating accessory the planter is as important as the foliage growing in it.

Sand art planters are a fascinating alternative to the standard clay pot. Each one is exciting, colorful, and a unique work of art. As long as the sand is nontoxic, the design will not harm the plant; and as long as it is colorfast, the colors will not run if water accidentally penetrates the sand.

Terrariums and cactus pots are especially well suited for sand art. In this chapter instructions are given for making these and other types of planters. Designs demonstrated are a landscape and a scalloped pattern. Also, many examples of planters are shown with a variety of sand art pictures and abstracts. Tips on caring for all sand art planters follow.

CACTUS POTS AND A SCALLOP DESIGN

Since cactus roots are small, cacti and succulents can be planted in almost anything—from a cylinder to a drinking glass. One interesting way to display cactus plants is inside a glass container that is only partially filled with sand designs and soil. This type of planter is a cactus terrarium.

The terrarium is a healthy atmosphere for cacti. Light shining through the glass walls stimulates growth, and startling patterns of development often appear within a few weeks after planting. The cactus planter demonstrated here is a terrarium. It is made with a tall "In-keeper" style cylinder from Libbey Glass and features skinny layers and a scalloping design.

Materials: Besides the cylinder, this project requires 2 or more cacti or succulents, 4 to 6 colors of sand including black and white, and cactus soil. Special cactus soil is generally available where you purchase the plants. If you prefer to mix your own soil, use one-third ordinary sand, one-third potting soil, and one-third vermiculite.

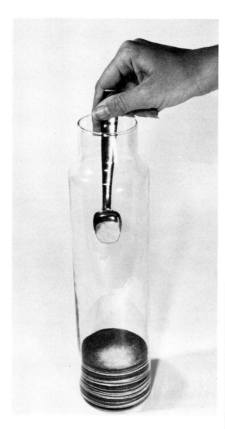

SKINNY LAYERING

Fill 1½'' to 2½'' of the cylinder with skinny layers. To keep the layers thin pour just enough sand in each color to barely coat the previous layer.

SCALLOP DESIGN

Cover skinny layers with a solid expanse of contrasting sand and two thin layers. Keep lines straight by smoothing with a paintbrush after each layer is poured. These thin layers are the bottom border of the scallop design. To make it stand out use black for the the lower outline with white sand above.

Poke through the top two layers with a pointed tool. Poke all around the container, making design points about 1'' apart.

Pour two more thin layers, using a new color with white again on top. Poke through the new layers 3 to 4 times between the original design points. Make the new design points deep enough to touch the white layer below.

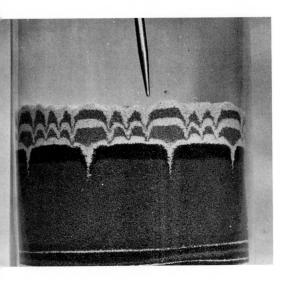

Build up the scallop design by repeating the last step. Use the same colors for the new layers.

Add white sand as needed to make the top layer even. Use a paintbrush to smooth top edges.

Finish the scallop pattern: First, add a thin black layer, and cover it with the color beneath the scallops. Then poke through all the layers, following the original design points in the lower border. To achieve a good separation between scallops, poke more than once if necessary.

Fill the cylinder with designs to 2″ to 6″ from the top. Here the scallop design is repeated and another inch of skinny layering is placed on top.

PLANTING

Spoon in 1″ to 2″ of cactus soil. Make a hole in the soil for each cactus plant.

Carefully remove each plant from its original container; shake off excess soil; and place it in the soil. Push extra soil over the roots. For decoration add pebbles or wood chips.

The finished cactus planter. Place it in a well-lighted area, but not direct sunlight; and add a small amount of water every 2 to 4 weeks.

The cactus pot comes in many shapes and sizes. Several examples, including cylinders, glasses, and plastic boxes, are shown on the next few pages. Some, as in the demonstrated project, have soil placed right on top of the sand design. Others have the soil hidden inside the last 1″ to 2″ of the design. The technique used for concealing soil is described on page 38.

SNIFTER WITH SCALLOPS. This brandy snifter uses only two colors of sand in another variation of the scallop design.

Cylinders make superb cactus planters. They have a generous area for sand art designs and ample room left for planting. Cylinders are available in many different heights and can be purchased in most department and variety stores. Make one or several. Together they work to complement one another.

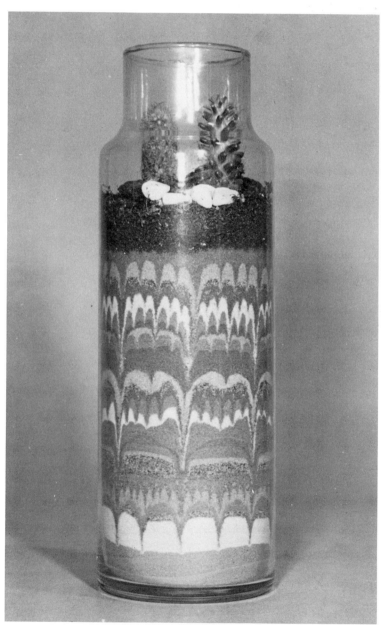

ABSTRACT CYLINDER. There is no regular pattern in this abstract design. The widths of layers vary, and the number of design points changes at different levels. Even the depth of design points varies within the same layer.

GEOMETRIC CYLINDER. A cactus terrarium with different geometric patterns top and bottom.

BUTTERFLY CYLINDER. A terrarium featuring a stylized butterfly, with deep purple outline and a pastel pattern on the wings.

Unusual shapes can be enlisted for cactus pots. A drinking glass, champagne glass, and plastic boxes make truly original planters. Look around your home for interesting containers. Perhaps you have an extra photo cube, parfait glass, or clear sugar bowl.

CITYSCAPE. Five ordinary plastic boxes were cemented together for this unique planter. The cityscape theme is carried throughout all the boxes. Each contains a city skyline composed of geometric-shaped buildings, with a full moon in the highest box.

SWIRL. This champagne glass was held on an angle as the first layers of sand were poured into the stem. With each layer the glass was shifted to a more vertical angle and turned slightly.

CLOUDS. Fluffy clouds and cactus in a Coca-Cola glass.

ART DECO CYLINDER. This abstract pattern has an art deco flavor. Here mounds are built up in thin layers with different patterns in each.

BRIDGE TERRARIUM. Just one unusual cactus plant is featured in this tiny terrarium. The design is a simplified bridge, with water below and a few birds above.

TERRARIUMS AND A LANDSCAPE DESIGN

Terrariums are fascinating. With practically no care at all a miniature garden will flourish inside a closed glass container. A sand design only adds to its beauty, whether the design is an inch tall or fills most of the container. The following project illustrates the principles of making a sand art terrarium. Also demonstrated is a landscape design, one of the most popular sand art subjects.

Materials: A terrarium requires drainage material, charcoal, terrarium soil, and miniature plants. For drainage material try gravel or small pebbles. Charcoal, which keeps the terrarium smelling sweet, can be purchased in chips at large florists or garden stores. Prepackaged terrarium soil is also available at the same sources. To mix your own soil combine one-third potting soil, one-third coarse sand, and one-third peat moss.

Many different plants will thrive in a terrarium. If you prefer not to cut back plants regularly, choose small slow-growing varieties. Use different shaped plants with varying colorations to make your garden more interesting. The number of plants you will need depends upon the size of your terrarium container.

Any large clear container will do. Make sure it has a cover and a wide enough opening for manipulating design tools. For this design use 4 to 5 sand colors including white, blue, and 2 to 3 earthy tones.

THE TERRAIN

Start the landscape with a natural, uneven terrain. Pour a wide band of white sand, a thin uneven streak of contrasting sand, and more white sand. Build up the land with additional streaks in one or two colors. Always leave the top edges somewhat uneven for a more natural look.

SNOWCAPPED MOUNTAINS

Spoon a mound of dark sand against one side of the container.

Cover the mound with a thin outline of white sand.

Form snowcaps on the mountaintop with short jabs of a pointed tool.

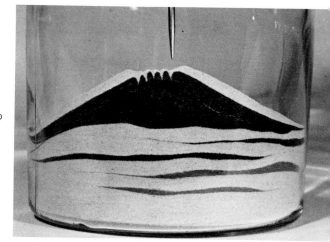

Spoon additional white sand over the mountain to rebuild the peak. Build similar mountains all around the container. Keep the center filled so that mountains do not erode while you work. Then top off the mountains with a blue sky.

BIRDS

Form two small side-by-side depressions in the sky above the mountains. Use any blunt tool, such as the wrong end of a knitting needle, to make the depressions.

Fill in the depressions with contrasting sand, letting the sand overflow slightly on both sides.

Poke a pointed tool between the now-filled depressions. This forms the bird's body, and separates the wings.

Cover with blue sand; and add more birds. Then bring the blue sand up to an even level all around the container.

CLOUDS: STRATUS

For each cloud add a thin uneven streak of white sand. To build up the sky cover with blue sand and add more white streaks.

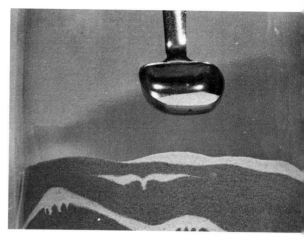

PLANTING

When your sand design is 1½″ to 3″ from completion, begin layering in terrarium materials. First, place a layer of drainage material in the container. Extend the layer to ¼″ to ½″ from the outside edges. The leftover space at the edges will be used for building up the sand art sky and clouds. Also put charcoal and soil in the center while finishing the design around the outside. First, place the charcoal layer over the drainage material; and then add the soil over it. When the sand design is completed, add an extra 1″ to 2″ soil.

Make holes in the soil for each plant. Lift each plant from its pot and gently shake the excess soil from the roots. Insert the plant into one hole, and add extra soil around the roots. Insert remaining plants; and as a decorative touch, place an interesting rock, wood chips, or pebbles around each plant.

The finished terrarium.

CARING FOR SAND ART TERRARIUMS

Before putting your terrarium on display, add a small amount of water. Pour slowly, keeping the water away from the container sides; and then cover the terrarium. Place it in a shady spot for a few days so that the plants can become accustomed to their new home. In the beginning check for condensation. A properly moist terrarium should have light condensation on the top and sides. If moisture is heavy, wipe the inside of the container and keep the cover off until the soil dries out. If no condensation appears, add a small amount of water.

When the moisture level is correct and the plants have adjusted to terrarium life, move the container to a lighted area. In general, terrariums require good light but not direct sunlight. They require little maintenance. Just check the moisture content periodically, adding a small amount of water whenever the condensation disappears.

FISHBOWL TERRARIUM. Simple contoured sand layers and a wide assortment of miniature plants turn an old fishbowl into an interesting sand art terrarium.

MASON JAR GARDEN. A terrarium with a simple, very basic sand art pattern.

CORKED TERRARIUM. This terrarium displays the previously demonstrated landscape in a smaller, narrower jar. (See pages 29–33.)

BOTTLE TERRARIUMS

The bottle garden is the most difficult type of terrarium to construct. To many who have tried to plant one, it seems the skill of a surgeon is needed to maneuver plants and materials through a bottle's narrow opening. For the same reason, making a sand art design in a bottle is more difficult.

If you wish to make a bottle terrarium, construct a long funnel by rolling up a sheet of paper. Use this funnel when adding sand and planting materials. For a planting tool tape a spoon to a long dowel. A straightened-out hanger is ideal for making designs in the sand.

BOTTLE GARDEN. This empty water bottle hosts a small abstract sand design and a simple arrangement of terrarium plants.

CHEATER. A more intricate design was easy to create in this water bottle. It is especially made by Riekes Crisa for use as a terrarium, with a large hole in back for people who prefer a simpler method of making a bottle garden.

OTHER PLANTERS

Besides cacti and terrarium plants, other types of greenery will also flourish in sand art planters. But since other plants require far more soil, you may wish to hide some of it inside the sand design. This way there is still room for substantial sand artistry. You can even fill the entire center of the planter with soil and have just a thin layer of soil showing on top. The procedure for making a full soil core is described here. This technique can also be used to layer vermiculite or other light materials into exceptionally large planters.

MAKING A SOIL CORE

Using a spoon bent into a ladle shape, place sand against all edges of the planter; and place a large mound of soil in the center.

Use the back of the spoon to push the soil toward the edges. Leave a margin of ¼″ to ½″ all around.

Build your sand design in this ¼″ to ½″ margin. As the sand design at the edge gets higher, add more soil to the center. Continue this procedure until the design is completed. Then top with a thin layer of soil.

HANGING CONE. Sailboats travel through a turbulent sand art sea in this cone-shaped hanging planter. Like all large sand art objects, this planter is quite heavy. To lighten it somewhat, vermiculite was layered into the center instead of sand.

←━━━

HANGING PLANTERS. These hanging bubble planters feature simple abstract patterns. To best show off the designs, minimal lucite and string plant hangers are used.

CUBE PLANTER.   A standard photo cube is the container for this spider plant. The sand design extends almost to the top edges, with soil throughout the core.

MINI-PLANTER.   A small plastic box is used as a tiny pot for ivy.

LANDSCAPE PLANTER. Another version of the sand art landscape, this time featuring a setting sun, mountains, and flowers.

CARING FOR SAND ART PLANTERS

The sand design is just an added attraction in cactus pots, terrariums, and all other planters. It does not help or hinder the growth of any plant. Each plant still requires the same amount of soil, sun, and water. Treat your plant as though the sand design were absent. To take care of your sand design, however, it is important not to overwater the plants. Always add water slowly and try to keep it away from the sides of the container. Use just enough water to moisten the soil, not the sand. If the design does get wet, do not water the plant again until the sand dries out. Then simply use less water next time.

SHELL VASE. Sand art and shellcraft are combined in this vase. Cowries, limpets, and Venetian snail shells are glued onto the recessed sections of a tall glass container; and a sand design is worked into the exposed center.

The sand design in this shell vase is built around one manufacturer's sand container. It is a plastic cylinder, almost as tall as the outside jar, with a 2″ diameter that leaves a generous ½″ all around for sand designing.

4
Floral Settings

Flowers, like plants, can be displayed in a variety of sand art settings. The natural, gentle look of a sand design is a beautiful complement to artificial, dried, or fresh flowers. In this chapter sand art is shown in vases, in a centerpiece, and with dried flowers under glass.

Choosing colors is especially important in a floral display. Think in terms of the finished piece when planning colors for your sand design. If you want a multicolored flower assortment, limit the number of colors in the sand design. Let the sand art enhance and not detract from the total look. As a general rule, use either flowers or sand for the main color interest.

VASES AND A GEOMETRIC DESIGN

In a vase plan the colors with your favorite fresh flowers in mind. You can always substitute similarly colored artificial flowers when you are between bouquets. By constructing the vase with an empty container inside, it is easy to change flowers when desired.

The size and shape of the central container determine the appearance of the sand art design and the vase's capacity for flowers. Ideally, it should be almost as tall and wide as the outside container, but be sure it is narrow enough to allow you to maneuver your sand art tools in the margin. Plastic cylinders, like the one used inside the shell vase, are perfect for wide containers. Test tubes are good for skinny-necked vases. Generally, hobby shops and chemical supply outlets stock test tubes in an amazing assortment of lengths and widths. This usually includes the right size for most slender vases.

The vase demonstrated here uses a test tube insert with an empty wine bottle outside. Its simple geometric pattern is adapted to the shape of the bottle. Instructions advise switching tools as the bottle begins to curve, and plain layering is called for where tools cannot touch the sides. If your container curves in different places, change the design if necessary and always use the tool that feels most comfortable.

Materials: Besides the wine bottle and test tube, this project requires 2 pointed tools and 3 or more sand colors. One tool must be straight and the other slightly curved. This way design work is possible against both straight and curving sections of the bottle.

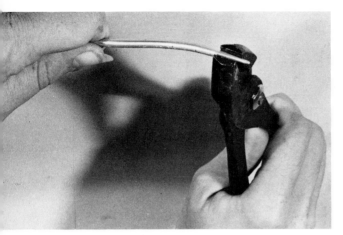

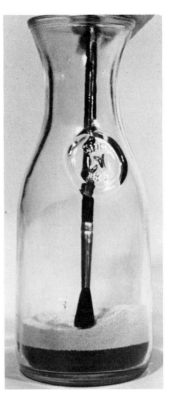

MAKING THE CURVED TOOL

Use pliers to bend a knitting needle or other pointed tool into a slight curve. Just the most gradual curve is all that is needed to reach the bottle's curving sections.

THE GEOMETRIC DESIGN

Pour even layers of sand in contrasting colors. In order to achieve the straight lines of the design, always use a paintbrush to smooth top edges before the next layer is poured.

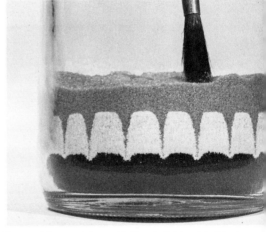

When you have three layers, make design points all around the container with the straight pointed tool. Each time poke through the top two layers, stopping as the tool barely touches the bottom layer.

Smooth top edges straight and level.

Pour a fourth layer of sand; and make new design points all around. Again, poke through the top two layers, this time centering new design points directly between previous ones. Then smooth top edges to complete the basic design; and cover with a thin layer of contrasting sand.

ADDING THE INNER CONTAINER

At about this point in the design insert the test tube. Gently press the tube into the sand until the top edges are flush with the bottle. A good time to place the tube in the bottle is when the distance between the sand design and the bottle's top edge is about ½'' less than the length of the test tube. If the design is not high enough yet, insert the test tube later.

Pour all remaining layers between the test tube and vase. If sand continually lands in the tube, place a tissue into the opening. Be sure it is loose, so that it comes out easily when the design is completed.

BUILDING UP THE DESIGN

Repeat the basic design in the same or different colors. Switch to the curved tool when the vase begins to narrow.

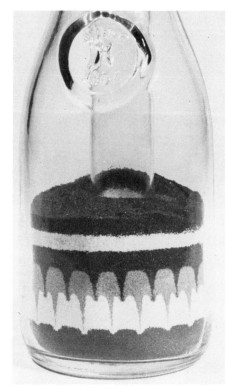

Fill container with level layers to 1½'' from the top.

Repeat the basic design with the straight tool. Then fill the vase with contrasting sand to within ¼'' from the top.

The finished vase, shown here with a fresh chrysanthemum. Put any type of flowers in your vase, dried or fresh. Insert flowers gently, and do not overstuff the vase. Pour water into the test tube, and try not to get the sand wet. For the best control, use a container with a pouring spout. When removing fresh flowers, use a large poultry baster to draw out the remaining water. Just squeeze the bulb, let go, and the water will be drawn inside the baster. Empty the baster, and repeat until all the water is gone.

TALL VASE. A relatively short test tube and a tall liqueur bottle make up this vase. Since the tube is almost as wide as the bottle's neck, design tools could not be used after it was inserted. But since the tube fills less than half the bottle, design work was possible before the tube was put in. Later, skinny layers were placed around it.

CRUET VASE. A sand art flower is always an appropriate subject for a vase. Originally, the embossed container for this vase came free with two packages of salad dressing.

DOUBLE DISPLAY. This two-sided cruet was discovered at a flea market. While being held at slightly changing angles, both sides were filled simultaneously with sand designs.

SLIM VASE. A modern, straight-sided vase with random sand patterns.

An insert is not necessary in a permanent floral display. Dried or artificial flowers can be placed in the sand after the design work is finished. To keep from disrupting the design, press each stem, one at a time, into the center of the vase. If a stem begins to poke through the side, just pull it back out and start again.

FLOWERS UNDER GLASS AND A FLORAL DESIGN

Another interesting floral display encloses flowers as well as sand art inside a glass container. It can be a cylinder, brandy snifter, or a more unusual shape. The shape of the container, the flower arrangement, and the sand design all combine to add interest to the finished display. The proportion of sand art to flowers is also important to flowers-under-glass projects. In most cases the display should be primarily flowers, with the sand as a complementary yet unobtrusive base. In the project demonstrated, a sparse assortment of dried flowers is placed in a floral sand design.

Materials: The container shown is a 9" Libbey brand cylinder with barber-pole cover. Sand colors are green, white, and any floral shade. Other materials for this project are Styrofoam, a cutting knife, dried or artificial flowers with firm stems, and coarse material to cover the sand design. Birdseed is used to top off this sand design. Other possible materials are gravel, pebbles, or crushed shells.

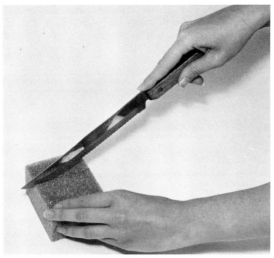

PREPARING FOR FLOWERS

Cut a Styrofoam block to fit inside the container. Leave ¼''
to ½'' margin at all corners. Make it ½'' shorter than the
proposed sand design. For this 9'' cylinder the block is
2½'' x 2½'' x 1½'' high.

Center the block in the container. All sand will be poured
between the Styrofoam and the container sides.

GRASS

Pour wide layers of green and white sand;
and poke all the way down to the bottom
with a pointed tool. Poke all around the
container at closely spaced intervals.

FLOWERS: STEMS AND LEAVES

Level an area of white sand with a paintbrush; and make a small depression in
the center. Use any blunt tool such as the
wrong end of a knitting needle, to create
this depression.

Fill the depression with green sand, letting the sand overflow on both sides.

Plunge the pointed tool through the now-filled depression. Make the design point long enough to touch the grass. This will turn the green sand into a stem with two leaves. Cover with more white sand, and make stems and leaves all around the container.

PETALS

Pour mounds of white sand between the stems; and fill the low areas with mounds of brightly colored sand. Each colorful mound should be V-shaped and centered over the stems.

Add a thin layer of white sand; and make a few shallow pokes in each flower. Smooth top edges with the paintbrush.

THE FLORAL ARRANGEMENT

Cover the sand design with a ½'' layer of birdseed or another coarse material: and insert flowers. Carefully press each flower into the Styrofoam. Root stems deeply in place. Cover the container.

The finished project, with orange sand art flowers to highlight the delicate orange coloring of the dried flowers.

DOUBLE-BUBBLE DISPLAY. The distinctive shape of this container determines the proportion of sand art to flowers. The bottom bubble is filled with sand art, while the top bubble encloses dried flowers.

SINGLE FLOWER DISPLAY. A very simple scallop design is featured in this brandy snifter. Unlike other flowers-under-glass designs, it displays a single puffy blossom.

FLORAL APOTHECARY JAR. A covered display combining sand art flowers and a dried arrangement. This time the sand art blossoms are set against a dark background.

THE FLORAL CENTERPIECE

A large Styrofoam block is the core for a floral centerpiece. It must be narrow enough for sand designing, and sufficiently tall to accommodate a generous assortment of dried flowers. To make a centerpiece place the Styrofoam block in a glass container. Let it protrude by 1½″ to 2″ above the container's top edge. Work sand designs in the margin between the Styrofoam and the glass. Then seal if desired, and insert flowers according to instructions.

SEALING THE SAND

Create a design around a large Styrofoam block and seal the sand design with a small amount of lacquer. Spoon on just enough lacquer to barely coat the sand. The lacquered top will be hidden by the flowers and it will keep the sand from shifting.

ARRANGING THE FLOWERS

Insert flowers into the protruding Styrofoam, one variety at a time. Begin with the largest flowers, and work symmetrically. In other words, put the first flower in the same position on all sides before going on to the second flower. Keep adding flowers until the arrangement is full; and then fill it in with accent flowers. The results can be fantastic.

CENTERPIECE.   The floral centerpiece, with a sand art base and an abundant flower arrangement.

5
Sandpaintings

Hundreds of years ago, long before glass jars existed commercially, Indians of the American Southwest were creating images in sand. Sandpainting has been used in religious ritual throughout the history of many southwestern tribes. For special ceremonies colored sands are gathered from nearby deserts and used by the medicine man to paint images on the ground. His paintings are of holy spirits, made by letting the sand pass through his fingers with great skill and control.

The paintings formed on the ground are temporary. They are created for the ceremony and destroyed shortly afterward. Until recently, no lasting form of Indian sandpainting existed at all. Today, however, permanent sandpainting is possible. A new method allows artists to make lasting, decorative sandpaintings. Besides traditional Indian designs, modern abstracts and simple nature themes are also interpreted in these paintings. Instructions in the permanent technique, along with different examples of Indian sandpainting, are shown in this chapter.

Also demonstrated is a type of sandpainting based upon modern three-dimensional principles. Using slim Plexiglas containers and glass and wood frames, the sand design is made as a painting that can be hung on a wall or displayed as a freestanding form.

HUNCHBACK YEI. Navajo sandpainting used for healing purposes. *Collection: The American Indian Arts Center, New York City*

INDIAN SANDPAINTING: THE PERMANENT TECHNIQUE

A simple butterfly figure is used here to illustrate Indian sandpainting. Any subject, regardless of complexity, can be made the same way. Some examples of modern and traditional subjects and other uses of sandpainting techniques follow.

Materials: For this type of sandpainting you will need several colors of sand, a plywood backing, paintbrushes, paper, carbon paper, and lots of newspaper to cover the work area. Also needed is a mixture of three parts white glue to one part water. This mixture is used for applying sand.

"PAINTING" THE BACKGROUND

Brush an even coat of the glue mixture onto the plywood. This even application is crucial for a smooth sand background and the success of the final painting. If desired, a background can also be made by cutting a sheet of sandpaper to size, and gluing it onto the wood.

Spoon sand over the entire surface of the wood.

Gently lift the wood, letting all but a thin layer of sand slide onto the newspaper. Firmly tap the wood in back. This will remove all remaining loose sand.

RETURNING THE SAND

Lift up the top sheets of newspaper and pour the sand back into its container. When the sanded background is dry, apply a second coat according to the preceding steps.

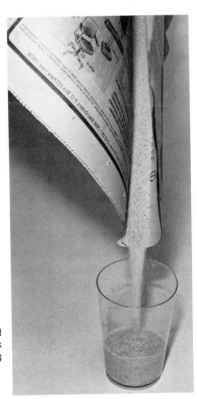

TRANSFERRING THE DESIGN

Using carbon paper, trace a picture onto the background. Ideally, the resulting lines should be dark enough to see, but light enough to be hidden eventually by the sandpainted design. If only a vague outline results from your tracing, lightly go over the lines directly on the background.

PAINTING THE DESIGN

Paint one outline with the glue mixture. To keep the line fine, use a small paintbrush to apply the mixture.

Cover the area with sand; and tilt the plywood to remove excess sand. Then tap it firmly on the back. This basic technique for applying sand is used for painting solid areas and remaining outlines. Finish your sandpainting according to this method and the general sandpainting rules that follow.

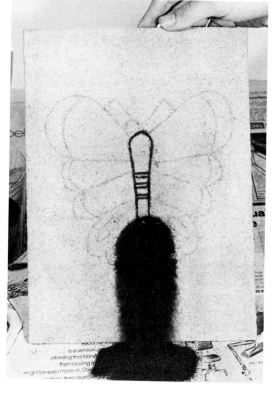

GENERAL SANDPAINTING RULES

1. "Paint" pictures according to the instructions on pages 58-60 and below.
2. Apply sand one color at a time. Finish all areas of the first color before going on to the next color. Let painting dry thoroughly between colors.
3. In general, paint outlines before solid sections. Paint the outline with a small brush, making as thin a line as possible.

4. Paint solid sections by applying the glue mixture to the guidelines, and then filling in the outlined shape.

5. Do not let the glue dry before covering the area with sand. For unusually large shapes paint small sections at a time.

6. To paint adjacent sections apply glue as close as possible to the next section. This prevents unnecessary spaces in the finished sandpainting.

7. When not in use, keep brushes in a cup of water. This will keep the bristles from stiffening between glue applications.

8. If desired, follow the same sandpainting rules for a second coat of sand. Let the painting dry thoroughly before the new coat is applied. In general, most sandpaintings require two coats.

Finish all areas of one color before applying the next color of sand.

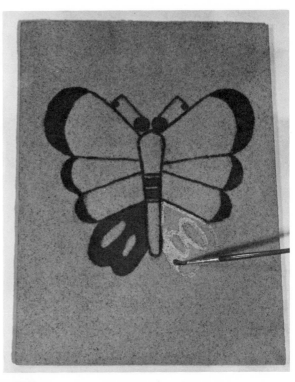

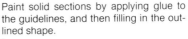

Paint solid sections by applying glue to the guidelines, and then filling in the outlined shape.

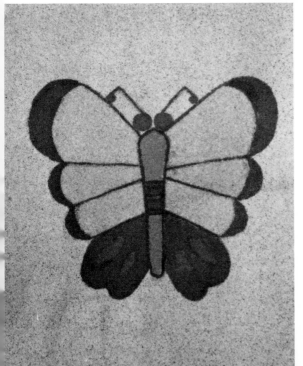

SANDPAINTING. The finished sandpainting, with a butterfly design.

TRADITIONAL SANDPAINTING

"Yei" figures and representations of the sun are traditional subjects portrayed in Indian sandpainting. The examples here illustrate these themes. All are ceremonial designs used for healing purposes.

SUN EAGLE. Navajo sandpainting. *Collection: The American Indian Arts Center, New York City*

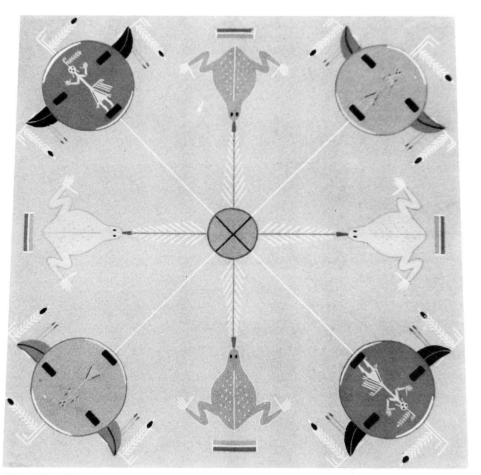

RELATED SUN EAGLES. Navajo sandpainting. *Collection: The American Indian Arts Center, New York City*

FIRE GODS. Navajo sandpainting. *Collection: The American Indian Arts Center, New York City*

CONTEMPORARY SANDPAINTING

One Navajo artist, David Chethlahe Paladin, uses the sandpainting technique to create modern abstract designs. His dramatic use of form and color separates his work from traditional Indian sandpaintings, and makes his paintings totally unique.

SPIRIT WORLDS.   David Chethlahe Paladin. Sandpainting. *Collection: The American Indian Arts Center, New York City*

PATTERNS OF THE UNIVERSE. David Chethlahe Paladin. Sandpainting. *Collection: The American Indian Arts Center, New York City*

THE SUN/THE MOON. David Chethlahe Paladin. Sandpainting. *Collection: The American Indian Arts Center, New York City*

SNAKE PRIEST. David Chethlahe Paladin. Sandpainting. *Collection: The American Indian Arts Center, New York City*

SANDPAINTED OBJECTS

Sandpainting techniques have many applications. Two examples other than pictures are shown here. There are additional possibilities as well. Just a few suggested items are jewelry, tabletops, and collage backgrounds.

SANDPAINTED MIRROR. A mirror decorated with a vibrant sandpainted border.

SANDPAINTED JEWELRY BOX. Here an empty wooden cigar box is converted into a one-of-a-kind jewelry box. The lid decoration was inspired by traditional thunderbird designs, and the border adapted from Navajo rug patterns.

Two cactus cylinders with abstract designs.

Seascape design. Modern, three-dimensional sandpainting in slim plastic frame.

Santa. A common ginger jar converted into a Christmas figurine.

A sand art terrarium table constructed of acrylic plastic.

A lamp made up of skinny sand layers and a chemical flask.

Shellcraft and sand art combined in a vase.

Flowers under glass. An apothecary jar filled with dried flowers and a floral sand design.

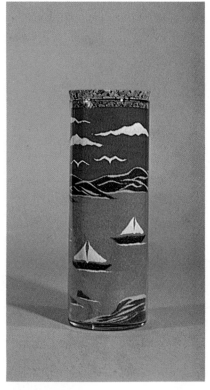

A decorative cylinder displaying a sailboat scene ''in the round.''

A sand art display case featuring an interesting assortment of shells.

Hunchback Yei. A traditional Navajo sandpainting used for healing purposes. *Collection: The American Indian Arts Center, New York.*

The Sun / The Moon. David Chethlahe Paladin. A contemporary sandpainting. *Collection: The American Indian Arts Center, New York.*

Flight. A freestanding, three-dimensional sandpainting on a contrasting base.

Another three-dimensional sandpainting framed in wood and glass.

A mason jar terrarium with a basic sand art pattern.

A colorful cactus terrarium in a tall cylinder.

A hanging cone planter combining sailboats, a mountain range, and a turbulent sea.

A cactus cylinder with a butterfly design.

A cityscape in a multilevel cactus planter.

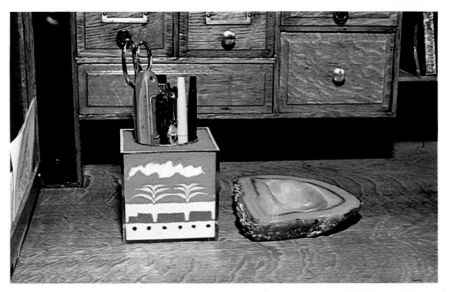

A handy utensil holder for desk, sewing table, or drawing board.

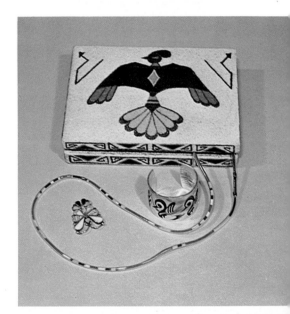

A sandpainted jewelry box. Note the sand art necklace of plastic tubing.

A face done in an egg-shaped container.

THREE-DIMENSIONAL SANDPAINTINGS AND A SEASCAPE DESIGN

It is the shape of the container that qualifies the next project as a sandpainting. It employs three-dimensional sand art techniques in a slim plastic frame, and has the overall appearance of a painting. Like other sand art objects, the finished painting is perfect as a freestanding form. Or else it can be treated as a classic painting and hung on a wall. The subject demonstrated is a seascape. Included are instructions for ocean waves, a full moon, and sailboat. If a two-sided picture is desired, work each step front and back. But be sure you do not pull design tools far back into the container before lifting them out of the sand.

Materials: Because of its unusual shape, the sandpainting frame must be constructed. To duplicate the frame shown, purchase ⅛″ acrylic as follows: 2 sheets 9″ x 11″ for front and back; and 2 strips 7″ x 1″ and 2 strips 9½″ x 1″ for the sides. Also needed are solvent cement and a special applicator. For designing sand in a frame of this size, use any long pointed tool. Bend the tool slightly if your frame is taller or narrower. To simplify the instructions sand colors are specified. These colors are white, black, orange, light and dark brown, and two shades of blue. However, if you prefer, other colors may be substituted.

To assemble the frame read the basic construction principles on page 107 to get a better understanding of how to work with acrylic sheets. Then sand the edges of the side strips to a satin finish, and buff the edges of the front and back sheets to a transparent finish. Cement three sides together, using two short strips and one long strip; sandwich the three-sided unit between front and back sheets; and carefully cement strips along the outside seams. If the painting is to be hung, drill two small holes in the back sheet before assembling the frame. Back the still-masked sheet with wood, and drill each hole approximately ½″ from each side and 1½″ to 2½″ from the top.

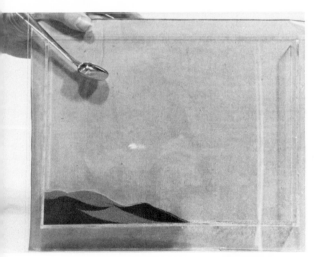

THE REEF

Alternately place mounds of dark and light brown sand into one side of the frame. *

* To make the frame more visible in these photographs the masking paper was left on the back sheet. It is not necessary to keep the paper on while you work.

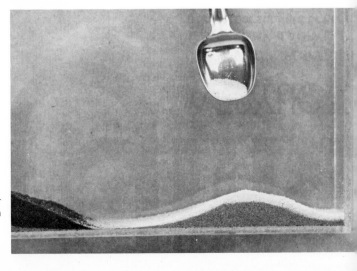

WAVES

Spoon a mound of blue sand in the other side of the frame; and cover it with a thin white line.

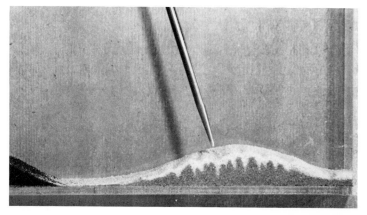

Poke into the blue mound with the pointed tool. This makes a white cap on the wave. For realism, vary the depth of each poke and the spaces between pokes.

Add a small amount of white sand to rebuild the white cap. Keep top edges somewhat uneven.

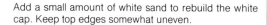

THE TURBULENT SEA

Build waves, one at a time, across the painting. Stagger the waves on top of one another; and leave a long depressed area in the center for the upcoming boat.

THE SAILBOAT

Fill in most of the long central depression with black sand. Smooth top edges with a paintbrush.

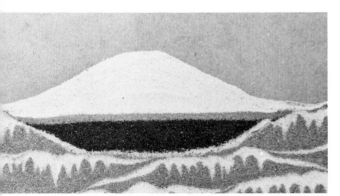

Cover the black sand with a thin line in the background color, in this case orange for the mountain; and top it with a mound of white sand.

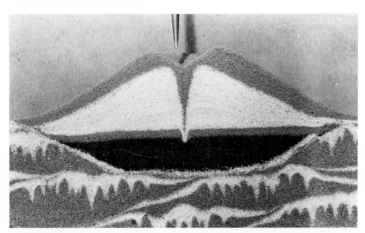

Completely surround the mound with the background color; and poke into the mound to make two sails. Use the pointed tool for the sails; and poke twice if necessary for a good separation.

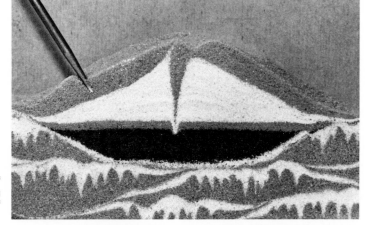

Steepen the diagonal sides of each sail by running the tool along the edges. Start at the base of each sail, and pull the tool upward.

THE FLAG

Use the paintbrush to form a long shallow depression above one sail. Make it about half the sail's length.

Fill the depression with white sand.

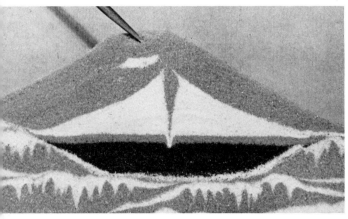

Cover the white sand with additional background color; and shape it into a flag with the pointed tool. To do so, gently run the tool along the top edges of the white sand.

MOUNTAINS

Shape the background color into a mountain. Use the paintbrush to make top edges irregular and natural-looking.

THE MOUNTAIN RANGE

Build mountains all across the painting; and cover mountaintops with an irregular cloud layer. Build mountains one at a time, in orange and two shades of brown. Make edges of each mountain irregular before adding the next mountain or topping with clouds.

A FULL MOON (OR SUN)

Add blue sand for the sky, preferably a different blue than the sea; and form a large semicircular depression with the paintbrush.

Fill the depression with a large mound of white sand.

Cover the mound with more blue sand; and round the sides with the pointed tool. Insert the tool into the blue sand, on the left side of the moon, and gently push toward the shape. The pressure of the blue sand will cause the side to flatten out and become rounder. Adjust the tool's angle to round upper and lower corners of the shape. Repeat on the other side; and fill the frame to the top with blue sand.

SEASCAPE SANDPAINTING. The finished painting, sealed in place with the top strip. Before sealing your painting, wait a few days for the sand to settle. Then add more sand if needed, and tape the top strip in place. Tape the top strip at the corners, and tighten the entire unit by running 2 to 3 pieces of tape over the top. Slowly turn the painting face up on a flat surface. If the sand starts to shift, stop turning immediately. Then stand the painting up again, remove the tape and top strip, and add more sand. When the painting is finally down flat, cement the top strip to the back sheet with solvent cement. Just by bonding this one seam, the top will stay on securely, and no cement will show in front.

TROPICAL SANDPAINTING. A palm tree bends seaward in this tropical sandpainting. In the background a bright yellow sun sets behind distant hills.

FREESTANDING PAINTING: FLIGHT.   A lone airplane climbs into the sky. Above, wispy clouds; below, hills, valleys, and moutain peaks.

GLASS AND WOOD FRAMED PAINTINGS

A sandpainting can also be framed in wood and glass. To make the frame shown, purchase wood as follows: 9″ x 12″ x ¼″ plywood; 2 strips ½″ x ½″ x 12″; 2 strips ½″ x ½″ x 8″; 4 framing strips with mitered corners, measuring ¾″ x 9″ x 12″ on the inside. Other materials needed are 9″ x 12″ x ⅛″ window glass, picture hooks and wire, 1½″ plastic tape, white glue, wood stain, and varnish. To prevent cut fingers have a glazier cut the glass to size and polish all edges.

ASSEMBLING THE FRAME

Glue side and bottom strips onto the plywood; and glue the glass sheet on top. Put the top strip aside. It will be used later to seal the finished sand design. If the picture will be hung, attach picture hooks before putting on the glass top. Attach picture hooks near the edges, and be sure screws go through both thicknesses of wood.

Tape outside edges to ensure against sand leakage. Let the tape overlap the glass front and plywood back. At this point you can make the sandpainting inside the frame. Fill the frame to ½″ from the top with the sand designs; and then seal the frame with the top strip. To seal the sandpainting wait a few days for the sand to settle; and then press the leftover strip in place. It is important that the top edges of the strip and frame are flush. If not, remove strip; and add or subtract sand as needed for a perfect fit.

Stain and varnish framing strips; and glue them around the finished and sealed sandpainting.

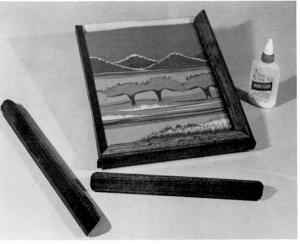

WATERSIDE SANDPAINTING. The finished sandpainting, framed in wood and glass. Since the frame is only ½'' deep, a slightly curved knitting needle is necessary for making the trees and grass.

6
Sand Art Sculptures

Sand art can be combined with plants or flowers, or used as furniture and paintings. But it is also beautiful all alone. Although the medium combines well with other elements, sand art does not need extra embellishments to justify its existence. Following this concept, the objects in this chapter have no foreign elements or practical purpose. They simply show sand art as it is—an exciting three-dimensional art form.

Since three-dimensional artworks are properly described as sculptures, any container filled with sand art is a sculptural form. Ordinary bottles and cylinders adapt well to this role. Each acts as a showcase for simple or elaborate designs. Unusual containers work well as representational forms, their shapes becoming an integral part of the sand art design.

In sculpture, skill and imagination count more than ever. Without flowers, plants, or purpose to distract from the finished object, the design stands by itself. But because usefulness is no consideration and there is nothing to compete with the artwork, freedom is unlimited in container choice as well as design. Sculpture, more than any other sand art form, affords a real opportunity for creative expression.

THE DECORATIVE CYLINDER

Cylinders are a wonderful way to show off sand art skills. Any design can be put inside—abstracts, simple pictures, or complex scenes. Sides are straight, allowing tools to reach every part of the container easily. And the cylindrical shape lets you plan a design with interest at every angle.

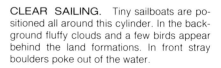

PATTERNED CYLINDER. A simple pattern composed of thin bands on a blue background. The design is sectioned off by three bands with long and short design points.

CLEAR SAILING. Tiny sailboats are positioned all around this cylinder. In the background fluffy clouds and a few birds appear behind the land formations. In front stray boulders poke out of the water.

WORDS, LETTERS, AND A "L-O-V-E" DESIGN

Individual letters or whole words can be written in sand. The same principles for sand art pictures apply to sand "scribing." As in any design, think of the message from the bottom up; and simplify letters as much as possible.

A relatively easy way of constructing a sand art message is by giving each letter its own plastic box. After all the letters are made, the boxes are placed together to spell out the word. This letter-by-letter method is demonstrated in the project below.

For ease, letters are stretched corner to corner and made on one side only. If you wish, turn stray colored sands on the other sides into a design. If you wish to have a two-sided message, reverse the letter order in back. In other words, back up the first letter with the last letter.

Materials: This project requires 4 plastic boxes to spell out the word "LOVE." Only 2 colors of sand are needed: white for the background and red for the letters. The boxes are available in plastic supply outlets, psychedelic shops, and many variety stores. Purchase boxes with tight-fitting lids, preferably black. This way the message will have a contrasting base when the boxes are turned upside down.

PREPARATION

Write out the message on a piece of paper for reference. Keep it in sight while you work. It will help you proportion the letters properly. For this project turn the paper upside down.

"L"

Fill slightly more than half of one box with white sand; and cover with a thin red layer.

Press into the right-hand side of the box with a pointed tool. Press several times until a substantial vertical line is formed. If the red sand begins to erode in the corners, add more as you work. Then smooth top edges with a paintbrush, and fill the box with white sand.

SEALING THE BOX

Cover the finished box. Line the lid with clay or putty if there is empty space between the sand and the lid.

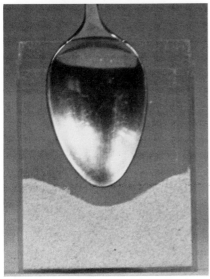

"O"

Fill about one-third of the box with white sand; and use a spoon to make a deep depression in the center.

Fill the depression with a red layer and a white mound.

Cover the mound with a red layer; and connect corners with the pointed tool. Press several times into both sides until wide lines are formed around a relatively circular center. Then smooth top edges with a paintbrush.

Fill the box with white sand; and cover as described for the letter "L."

Cover with a red layer; and use a
paintbrush to form a point.

"V"

Pour a mound of white sand into the
third box; and shape the top edges
into a point.

Fill the box with white sand; and cover
as described for the letter "L."

"E"

Fill about one-fifth of the box with
white sand; and cover with a red layer,
white layer, and an especially thin red
layer. Use a paintbrush to straighten
top edges before pouring new layers.

Press the pointed tool into the right-
hand side of the box. Press several
times, until a wide line connects both
red layers. Then smooth top edges
with the paintbrush.

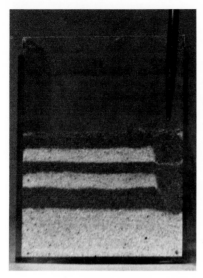

Pour a white layer; pour a red layer; and connect the new red layer to the middle red layer with the pointed tool. Then smooth top edges.

Fill box with white sand; and cover as described for the letter "L."

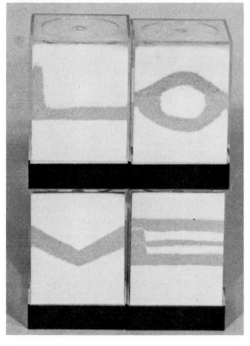

LOVE LETTERS IN THE SAND. The finished project, with boxes turned over and set up in two different ways—side by side in the classic way and arranged as a modern sculptural form.

TURNING THE BOXES UPSIDE DOWN

Turn each box over slowly, watching carefully for shifting sand. If the sand begins to shift, there is empty space between the sand and the lid. If so, stop immediately, reopen the box, and add more clay or putty to the lid. Then cover the box and try again. When the box is properly filled, no sand will move as the box is turned over.

REPRESENTATIONAL FORMS

In representational sand sculptures the design is interlinked to the container's shape. Ideally, when the artwork is finished, the sculpture should look like a particular subject. Sometimes a container seems to have been designed for the sand art subject. Most often, however, an exact shape will not be found, and the container will bear only a vague resemblance to the subject in mind. In these cases the sand art makes the subject work. All it takes is sand art know-how and an ability to see a subject in an empty container. With these qualities and the right colors of sand, a vague resemblance can often turn into a remarkable likeness.

THE FACE AND MAKING FACIAL FEATURES

There are many appropriate jars for the sand art face, and as many ways of designing facial features. This project uses an egg-shaped container to demonstrate one method of making the face.

Materials: Aside from the container, tools, and sand in facial colors, have white glue on hand to seal sand in the hat. Where sand colors are specified in the instructions, they can be changed according to individual preferences. Here the face is pink with features in red, white, and black, and a hat in red and blue.

LIPS

Pour a wide layer of pink sand; and make a small depression with the tip of a teaspoon.

Fill most of the depression with a mound of red sand; and cover with a thin pink line. Push gently at the corners of the mound with the wrong end of a paintbrush. This lowers the corners slightly, and gives the lower lip a more graceful shape.

Add a red mound slightly wider then the lower lip; and poke into the mound with a pointed tool. If the mound is too straight at the sides, brush some sand away from each corner. Otherwise, the mouth will look too sad.

CHEEKS AND NOSE

Cover the lips with pink sand; and make three depressions in the sand. Use the spoon to form the depressions. Make one depression over the mouth, and smaller depressions on each side.

Fill small depressions with red mounds; and add a thin black line to the center depression. Use a paintbrush to thin out the black line.

Cover all mounds with pink sand; and shape them into a nose and cheeks. To shape, insert the pointed tool between the nose and one cheek. Gently press the tool toward either shape. The pressure of the pink sand will cause the side to flatten. Make it rounder by changing the tool's angle, and pressing toward the upper and lower corners. Use this technique to round both cheeks and both corners of the nose.

EYES

Bring pink sand to an even level all around; and make two depressions for eyes. Use the spoon to form the depressions.

Fill each depression with a thin black line and a white mound.

Cover each mound with a wide band of black sand; and make pupils by poking into the white mound. Use the wrong end of a paintbrush for the pupils. Then add more black sand to rebuild the band; smooth top edges with a paintbrush; and brush away any black sand between the eyes.

Cover the eyes with pink sand; and poke into the black band with the pointed tool. Then fill the container to the top with pink sand.

THE HAT

Fill the glass cover with an irregular contoured pattern. Contour each layer with a paintbrush before the next layer is poured. To keep the cover steady while you work, place it in a clear plastic cup.

Seal in the sand with a mixture of white glue and sand. Stir sand into glue until a thick, pasty consistency is achieved. Then pour just enough into the cover to coat the sand's top edges. No more is needed. Its purpose is to keep the sand in place when the hat is turned upside down. Too much of the mixture will be too obvious.

SAND ART FACE. The finished project, with hat in place. When the glue and sand mixture set, the hat is simply turned over and put on the finished face.

BOY'S FACE. This head was made upside down in a large bubble flask. Bent tools were used to reach into the bubble, and a small amount of lacquer sealed the sand in at the neck.

MR. SANDMAN. The hatlike bottle cap determined this bottle's destiny. The embossed area provides a natural boundary for the shirt section, and the clear area above has just enough room for a face.

SANTA. This container is a plain ginger jar, sold in most variety stores all year round. A friend's comment that the jar resembled Santa is responsible for its present form.

CHRISTMAS TREE. With or without sand, this container is a Christmas tree. The sand art colors it green and gives it rows of tinsel and ornaments.

DISPLAY CASES AND A MUSHROOM DESIGN

Sand art is a unique setting for natural elements on display. Simple layering or a pattern carrying through the display theme adds to the subject's beauty. Driftwood, shells, or a pinecone arrangement would all look lovely in a sand art display case. A wild mushroom discovered on a Massachusetts farm is featured in the following project. It is made with a 6" plastic cube and a sand art mushroom design.

Materials: Special requirements for this project are a short pointed tool; coarse material to cover the design, such as pebbles, gravel, or crushed shells; and a natural element to fill the display. The plastic cube can be purchased at many florists, variety stores, and plastic supply outlets. If you wish to construct your own case, instructions are given on page 107 for a 16" cube. Purchase ⅛" acrylic and adapt the instructions to a 6" size. Five to seven colors are used in this design, including green, black, and white.

THE GROUND
Alternate light streaks with dark, uneven layers. Here and throughout the project repeat the design on the opposite side of the cube; and reverse the design on adjacent sides.

MUSHROOM STEM
Place a green mound in one corner of the cube and another slightly off center; and add a black mound between them.

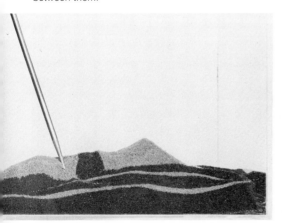 

Shape the black mound into a mushroom stem. To shape, insert the pointed tool ¼" to ½" to the left of the black mound. Gently push toward the mound, and straighten the side with an upward motion. Run the tool along the edges, tilting the side slightly inward. Repeat on the right side.

GRASS
Pour white sand over the green mounds; and poke into the green sand with the pointed tool. Poke halfway through the sand at closely spaced intervals.

MUSHROOM: UNDERSIDE

Add white sand on both sides of the stem; making the white sand slope upward from the stem. Make the slope steeper on the side closest to the center of the cube.

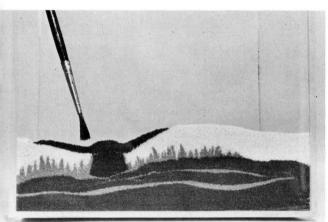

Place a black line in the depression, with extra black sand over the stem. Use a paintbrush to smooth the line.

Add shallow contrasting mounds on each side of the stem; and place a black mound on the stem.

Shape the black mound into the stem top, following the original angles of the stem. Keep a sand-filled spoon handy in case the side color erodes as you work. If sides get too thin, sprinkle on more sand.

Add extra sand over sides and stem; smooth top edges with a paintbrush; and cover with a black line.

Poke into the mushroom's underside with a short pointed tool. Angle design points toward the stem; add extra black sand if necessary; and then smooth top edges with a paintbrush.

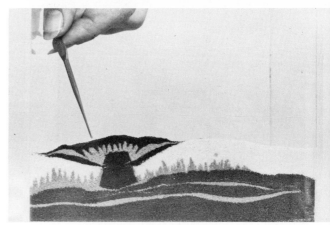

MUSHROOM: CAP

Add a mound of sand for the cap. Then brush away excess sand in the corners.

Cover the mound with white sand; and shape it into a mushroom cap. To shape place the pointed tool near the bottom corner of one mound. Press against the mound with an upsweeping motion. Run the tool along mound edges until the sides have a steeper, more realistic look. Repeat on both sides. Then bring white sand to an even level; and cover with coarse material.

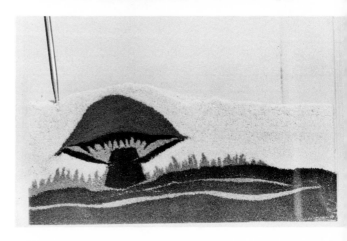

MUSHROOM DISPLAY. The finished display case, enclosing a real mushroom and sand art in a mushroom theme.

SHELL DISPLAY. A display case featuring a shell arrangement in a setting of crushed shells and sand. The crushed shells are layered into the cube, and top off the sand design.

7
Sand-around-the-House

Sand art can make dramatic furniture and home accessories from otherwise ordinary bottles and cubes. Colorful candle holders, serving pieces, utensil holders, lamps, tables, and a truly unique fishbowl are all included in this chapter. Except for the fishbowl, which was purchased at a pet shop, every home accessory was made with flea market bargains or discards from deep inside the closet. The tables were constructed from acrylic sheets according to principles described later on.

The tables are simple to build, and it is easy to find interesting bottles, plates, or cruets for accessory projects. Do not limit yourself to the exact projects shown. Many of the components will not be available at your particular sources. All items shown are just examples of what can be done with sand art and some throwaways.

For these projects more than any others, look critically before throwing things away. If it is clear, it is probably useful. Even if you can't duplicate many projects in this chapter, the castoffs you find may be the inspiration for accessory ideas of your own.

THE FISHBOWL AND A SHELL DESIGN

Although a standard goldfish bowl is used here, any large clear container will work for the fishbowl project. Just make sure it is roomy enough for the goldfish. This bowl features a stylized shell design against a background of blue sand. After the design is completed, water is slowly syphoned into the bowl. The water will seep into the sand, but it will not change the design. Dirt will eventually seep into the sand. To prevent this from happening too rapidly, change the water frequently with a syphon pump.

The fishbowl is not a permanent project. Even with proper care, it will not last indefinitely. But it is one of the most striking applications of sand art and a wonderful conversation piece for as long as it lasts.

Materials: For this project you will need a fishbowl, aquarium gravel, syphon pump, and 3 to 5 colors of sand. Be absolutely certain your sand is nontoxic and colorfast. A good idea is to purchase aquarium sand at the fish shop. Syphon pumps are often available at auto supply stores as well as aquarium shops. For design work a short pointed tool is also required.

SHELLS

Pour blue sand into the fishbowl; and create two deep depressions with a teaspoon. Here and throughout the design repeat on both sides of the bowl.

Fill each depression with a mound of light-colored sand.

Cover each mound with a layer of contrasting sand (*left*); and then use a short pointed tool to poke lines into the mounds (*right*). To angle the lines aim the tool toward the mound's bottom.

Build up shells with additional layers: Each time add a new layer (*left*); and then poke the tool into the layer below. Always follow the original design points and angle.

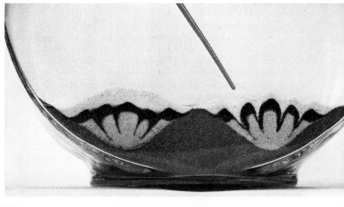

After 2 to 4 shell layers are added, cover both shells with blue sand. Then poke into the top shell layer; and smooth top edges with a paintbrush.

ADDING GRAVEL

Add a heavy layer of aquarium gravel; and put the fishbowl aside for 24 hours. At same time put aside a separate container with enough water to fill the fishbowl. After a day has passed, the sand will have settled somewhat, and the water will be suitable for the fishbowl.

ADDING WATER

Use a syphon pump to transfer the water into the fishbowl. Elevate the water container on a box or platform; insert the tube into the container; and squeeze the pump to start the flow of water into the fishbowl. Do not discard the remaining water when the fishbowl is full. After a short while the water will seep into the sand, and more water will have to be added.

FISHBOWL.   The finished bowl, with the goldfish inside.

UTENSIL HOLDERS AND A TRAIN DESIGN

An attractive holder for pencils, paintbrushes, sewing supplies, or even sand art tools can be made with a can and cube. The can is placed inside the larger clear cube, and sand designs are worked into the margin. The designs demonstrated here are a sand art train, stylized trees, and cumulus clouds. At the top the margin is covered with sandpainted cardboard.

Materials: This project uses a standard plastic photo cube and a clean empty 6-ounce fruit can. The can is almost as tall as the cube, with a diameter that leaves plenty of room between the containers for manipulating sand art tools. In this project and any others using inner and outer containers, these proportions are essential.

For the design a flat squared-off tool such as a flat coffee stirring stick is needed. Use 4 to 5 sand colors including white, blue, and yellow or light green. For the cover: cardboard, carbon paper, white glue, felt pen, paper, straight edge, and scissors are also required. To give the finished jar a more professional look, brush a coat of paint inside the can before beginning.

INSERTING THE CAN/STARTING THE TRAIN WHEELS

Place white sand in the cube; and place the can on top. Use as much sand as needed to make the top edges of both containers flush. Then use a paintbrush to make six small depressions. Here and throughout the design repeat each step on all sides of the cube.

Fill each depression with a mound of dark sand.

Cover with white sand; and shape the dark sand into wheels. To shape, insert a thin tool between two wheels, and gently push toward one of them. This will flatten the side. Change the angle of the tool as needed to make them rounder. Repeat on both sides of each wheel. Then smooth top edges of the white sand.

THE TRAIN CARS

Add an even layer of dark sand, and cover with white sand.

Separate cars by poking with a pointed tool. Poke between each pair of wheels as many times as necessary for a good separation. Turn the corner of the cube toward you to separate the corner cars. This way you can watch both cars as you poke. For the locomotive, press above one end car with a flat, blunt tool. If top edges of train cars are no longer level, gently press down above the raised areas with a flat, blunt tool. Then smooth top edges of the white sand.

TREES

Add three mounds of blue sand for sky; and fill the resulting depressed areas with yellow or light green sand. Let this sand slightly overlap the depressions on each side. These shapes will become the tree's lowest branches.

Poke into the center of each branch with the pointed tool. Poke tool. Poke deep enough to touch the white sand below.

Repeat the last two steps, this time making the branch shapes slightly shorter at the sides. Poke deep enough to touch the branches below.

Repeat the previous step for the next branches, making the new branch shapes even shorter than the last branches. Then cover the new branches with blue sand.

CLOUDS: CUMULUS

Use a paintbrush to form irregular contours in top edges; and place an irregular white shape on top. Then cover with more blue sand.

Insert the pointed tool behind the white shape, approximately ¼″ from the edge of the cube; and then run the tool from one end to the other. Repeat 2 or 3 times. This will distort the white shape and soften the edges, giving the shape a fluffy, cloudlike appearance. Then fill the cube to the top with more blue sand.

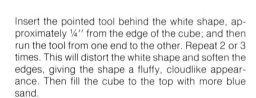

MAKING A COVER

Trace the shape for the cover onto a white piece of paper. Trace the outside edge of the can and the inside edge of the cube; and then transfer this pattern to the cardboard with carbon paper. An accurate pattern is crucial for a snug-fitting cover. When the pattern is transferred, cut out the shape.

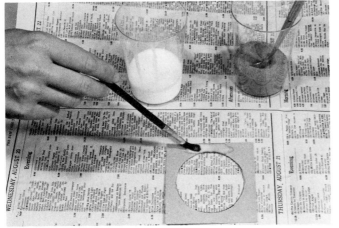
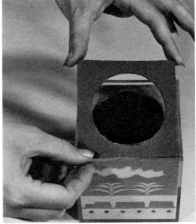

Paint the cardboard shape with a 3:1 mixture of white glue and water. Then spoon on blue sand, and lift the cardboard to remove the excess sand. When dry, apply a second coat of sand if needed. Again, let the cover dry.

Press cover between cube and can.

UTENSIL HOLDER.   The finished project, filled with pens, pencils, and other desk needs.

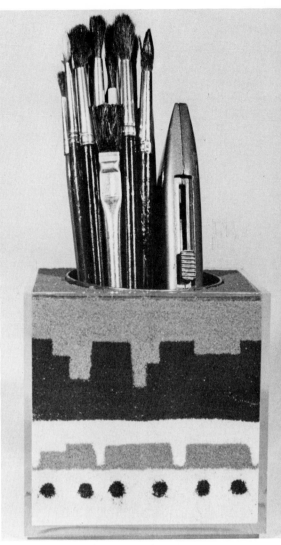

UTENSIL HOLDERS. Sand art trains also appear on these sewing supply and paintbrush holders. One train is set against mountain scenery while the other passes through the city.

FLASK LAMP.   This lamp is made with a flask from a chemical supply outlet.
The design is very simple, with just skinny layers in a multitude of colors.

LAMPS

Empty bottles and jugs have traditionally been used by home craftsmen to make inexpensive lamps. Now sand art adds a new dimension to this type of lamp. Simple layers alone can make any lamp far more interesting. In fact, layering is probably the best design technique for sand art lamps, Whether layers are skinny and even, or wide and free-form, you can have a beautiful lamp without manipulating tools through tiny bottlenecks.

If bottlenecks are especially narrow, it is often helpful to pour sand through a funnel. A long paper funnel, made by rolling up a sheet of newspaper, is an excellent way to pour the sand. For best results make the funnel fairly narrow throughout. To control the sand flow let the funnel almost touch the bottom of the bottle. Continue funneling in different colored sand until the bottle is filled.

Wire the lamp when the sand designs are finished. Only the simplest method of electrifying is used here. The socket, wire, and plug are purchased as one complete unit called an "instant," or "minute," lamp kit. The base of the unit is just placed into the mouth of the bottle with all wires outside.

An "instant" lamp, available at large hardware stores, is used to electrify this sand art lamp. The unit is placed in the container after the design work is completed.

JUG LAMP. An empty California white wine bottle is the base for this sand art lamp. The jug's light green tint was used to advantage, accenting the greens in the wide, uneven sand layers inside. The shade on top, like many available in variety stores and specialized lamp shops, clamps right onto the light bulb.

CANDLE HOLDERS

There are many ways of making a sand art candle holder. A candle can be inserted in a sand-filled bottle, as in the candle holder opposite. Or candles can be placed inside a glass container, with just enough sand art to keep the candle steady. As a safety precaution, be sure the container can withstand heat, and all parts of the container are a safe distance from the candle flame.

"SHRIMP/ICER" CANDLE. A unique candle holder, featuring sand art animals on parade. Originally a two-piece shrimp server, the candle was poured in the shrimp dish top and the sand design worked into the "icer" bottom.

HURRICANE CANDLE HOLDER. This container provides a natural boundary for the sand design. There is a geometric design in the straight-sided base, and a slim taper candle under the curving top.

BUBBLE CANDLE. A chunky bubble container with a wide candle.

CANDLE HOLDER. Sand art adds new interest to the chianti bottle candle holder. This lightly tinted bottle is filled with an easy layered design.

STACKED SERVER. Two platters separated by a sand-filled cruet.

CAKE PLATES. Simple bands of color are featured in the sand designs for both cake plates. One is supported by a discarded bud vase; the other uses a cruet.

SERVING PIECES

Here is one place empty cruets come in handy. As long as salad dressing makers continue to give away cruets with their product, you will always be able to find good, free bases for serving pieces. If you do not enjoy the dressings, perhaps a flea market has something for you. In fact, that is where all the plates and the skinny cake-plate base came from.

THE TERRARIUM TABLE AND CONSTRUCTING A CUBE

If it is large enough, a sand art terrarium can also be a table. The container is filled with sand designs and plants, as in any other sand art terrarium. The only requirement is that the cover, or tabletop in this case, be flat and removable.

The table shown here is a 16¼'' cube with a 20'' top. It is made from Plexiglas ® acrylic sheets according to directions on the following pages. These directions are very basic and can be adapted to almost any size cube or rectangle. By changing the size of the plastic sheets, you can make planters, display cases, sandpainting frames, and any other sand art containers using these same principles. The result will be exactly the shape you want, at a much lower price than ready-made versions.

Acrylic sheets, cut to your specifications, can be ordered from plastic supply companies. Directions are given here for preparing and assembling these precut pieces. If you wish to avoid the preparation stages, have the plastics company finish the edges for you. You can even have them assemble the container, but each added step increases your cost. On the other hand, if you prefer to cut your own pieces, check the Supply Sources section for booklets available from Rohm and Haas, the manufacturer of Plexiglas ® acrylic.

Materials: For the table shown purchase ¼'' acrylic sheets as follows: 4 sheets 16'' x 16'' for the sides; one 16¼'' x 16¼'' sheet for the bottom; one 20'' x 20'' sheet for the top; and 2 strips 15½'' x 1'' for holding the top in place. If you are having the edges finished by the plastics supplier, have them buff all edges of top and bottom sheets, 2 adjacent edges of side sheets, and all but one long edge of each strip. All other edges should have a satin finish.

Other necessary materials are solvent cement; cement applicator; masking tape; and ruler. To finish edges yourself, you will also need a drill with special buffing attachment; 150 to 320 grit wet or dry sandpaper, 400 to 500 grit wet or dry sandpaper; and a table clamp.

FINISHING THE EDGES

Clamp one sheet to a table; scrape the top edge with the back of a hacksaw blade or sharp knife to remove saw marks; and sand to a satin finish. Use increasingly finer grits from 150 to 320 grit wet or dry sandpaper. Repeat on all edges; and continue sanding with finer grits of 400 to 500 for all edges to be buffed. The satin finish assures a lasting bond on edges to be cemented, and improves the appearance of buffed edges.

Buff the edges that will be exposed in the finished cube. For the table project this includes all edges of the bottom piece and two adjacent edges on each side piece. For the tabletop buff both short ends and one long edge of each strip, and buff all edges of the top. To buff, clamp the piece to the table; apply buffing compound to the buffing wheel; and buff to a transparent finish.

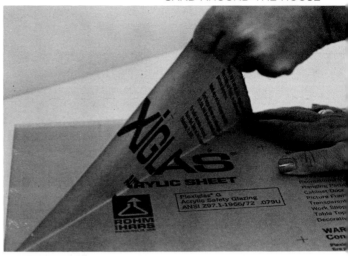

UNMASKING SHEETS

When all outside edges have been buffed, and all edges to be cemented are satin-smooth, peel off the masking paper. To prevent unwanted scratches, place each uncovered piece on a soft towel until it is ready for use.

ASSEMBLING THE CUBE

Tape the cube together. Start by taping two side pieces together. Have buffed edges on top and outside; and have satin edges on the bottom and butting against the adjacent sheet. Add all side sheets in exactly the same way; and then attach the bottom piece.

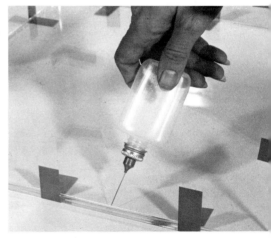

Join seams with solvent cement. Always have the edge to be cemented horizontal; and cement the seam from the inside. Turn the container on its side to cement the side seams. When seams are secure, remove the tape. Wait until the next day and fill it with sand art designs.

MAKING THE TABLETOP

Join strips to the top sheet. First test to see th strips will fit into the assembled cube. Then tap each strip exactly 2¼'' from three sides. Whe the top is on the table, these strips fit inside th cube and keep the top in place. Cement end remove tape when the bond is secure; and c ment the entire seam.

TERRARIUM TABLE. The finished cube, with the tabletop in place. Inside, the cube is filled with a scenic sand design and a miniature garden.

A CHECKERBOARD TABLE AND FILLING A TABLETOP WITH SAND ART

Another type of sand art table uses a deep tabletop filled with sand. This one is constructed of acrylic sheets and made into a checkerboard. Directions are given here for the checkerboard design, along with assembly instructions. It is advisable to read the directions for the cube table on page 107 before you begin. These directions include background information for working with acrylic sheets, and instructions for finishing the edges at home.

Materials: For this project you will need ¼″ acrylic sheets cut to the following sizes: 2 sheets 12½″ x 12½″ for top and bottom; 4 strips 2″ x 12¼″ for the sides; and 4 tubes 12″ × 2″. All edges of top and bottom sheets and one short end of each side strip should be buffed to a transparent finish. All other edges should have a satin finish. Other necessary materials are a utility knife; straightedge ruler; spray or liquid acrylic paint and brush; solvent cement; cement applicator; and 20 pounds of sand.

THE CHECKERBOARD TOP

Measure a ¼″ border on one acrylic sheet; and measure eight rows of eight 1½″ squares inside.

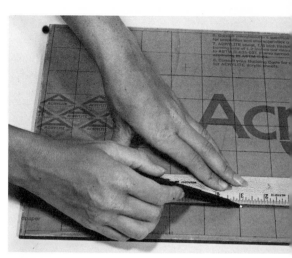

Using a utility knife and straightedge, cut through the masking paper along all ruled lines. Press lightly on the knife to prevent making deep scratches in the plastic. Light lines will be hidden by the paint.

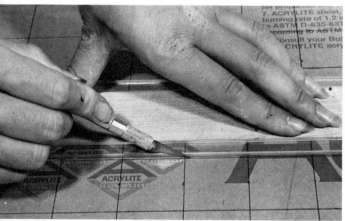

Peel away every other square of masking paper. Here, for demonstration purposes, the bottom sheet of masking paper has already been removed. For your table leave the bottom sheet attached until the top is ready for assembly.

Fill in every unmasked square with paint. Use spray paint or brush it on.

When the paint dries, peel off all remaining masking paper on the top sheet, bottom sheet, and side strips.

ASSEMBLING THE TABLETOP

Attach side strips to the checkerboard top. First place the checkerboard top, painted side up, on a soft cloth. Then tape *three* sides onto it, with buffed ends outside and satin-smooth edges butting against adjacent edge. Join all seams with solvent cement.

Join top and sides to bottom sheet. Since the tabletop is slim, carefully apply cement along the outside seams. When seams are secure, remove the tape. Wait until the next day before filling with sand designs.

FILLING THE TOP WITH SAND ART

Fill the tabletop with sand art designs. Turn the open side up, and use colors that contrast with the painted squares. This tabletop uses four different colors and a quantity of well-mixed waste sand as a fifth color. Here a simple layering pattern is used. Sand is spooned into the table in broken uneven layers, varying in height and length.

SEALING THE TABLETOP

Cement the last strip into place. First, wait a few days for the sand to settle and then place the strip on top. Add or subtract sand to fit. A *perfect* fit is extremely important. This will keep the design intact when the tabletop is turned over. When you are satisfied with the fit, tape the strip on top, and cement the short ends and back seam. Then turn the tabletop face up. This time and any time the table is moved or turned, move it slowly and set it down gently. Cement the last seam with the tabletop face up. Hold a tissue beneath the applicator tip to catch accidental drippings, if any.

JOINING LEGS

Cement legs to table with checkerboard facing down. Position legs in corners, at least ½" from outside edges.

THE CHECKERBOARD TABLE. The finished project. A handy table for a game of chess, or for an ashtray or telephone when the game is over.

Supply Sources

GENERAL SAND ART SUPPLIES:

Terrarium Town
123 West 28th St.
New York, N.Y. 10001

Agroth, Inc.
39 West 29th St.
New York, N.Y. 10001

SAND ART KITS:
Avalon
95 Lorimer St.
Brooklyn, N.Y. 11206

COLORED SAND:

Clifford W. Estes Company, Inc.
Box 105
Lyndhurst, New Jersey 07071
   Write for names of local dealers.

Activa Products, Inc.
582 Market Street
San Francisco, California 94104

GLASS CONTAINERS:

Riekes Crisa Corporation
General Offices:
P.O. Box 1271, Downtown Station
Omaha, Nebraska 68101
   Terrariums of all sizes and shapes, and
   decorator pieces.
   Write for names of local dealers.

Special Markets Department
Libbey Glass
Owens-Illinois, Inc.
P.O. Box 919
Toledo, Ohio 43693
   Cylinders, eggs, apothecary jars, and
   other novelty shapes.
   Write for names of local dealers.

Federal Glass
Division of Federal Paper Board Co., Inc.
Columbus, Ohio 43207
  Unique, decorative shapes.
  Write for names of local dealers.

PLASTICS:

Plexiglas ®
Rohm and Haas Company
P.O. Box 9730
Department JC
Philadelphia, Pennsylvania 19140
  Send 50¢ for distributor list, "Do It Your-
  self with Plexiglas," and other booklets,
  and mail-order form for tools and ac-
  cessories.

Industrial Plastics
309 Canal Street
New York, N.Y. 10013

Almac Plastics, Inc.
47-42 37th St.
L.I.C., N.Y. 11101

SPECIAL CONTAINERS:

Conso-Lab Supply Company
425 Merrick Avenue
Westbury, New York 11590
  Test tubes and chemical flasks.
  Write for brochure. $10 minimum on mail
  orders.

Index

B

birds, sand art, 31
bottle terrariums, 36–37

C

cactus pots, 19–28
candle holders, 104–5
care for sand art objects
    general principles, 18
    planters, 41
    terrariums, 34
centerpiece, floral, 55–56
checkerboard table, 109–12
clouds, sand art, 27
    cumulus, 99
    stratus, 32
construction projects
    checkerboard table, 109–12
    glass and wood frames, 76–77
    plastic cube, 107–9
    plastic frame, 69

D

design points, 10–12
design tools, 2–4
designs
    face, 84–87
    flower, 49–52
    general principles, 8–15
    geometric, 43–46
    landscape, 29–33
    L-O-V-E, 80–83
    mushroom, 89–92
    scallops, 19–23
    seascape, 69–74
    shells, 42, 93–96
    train scene, 97–101
display cases, 89–92

E

erosion, prevention of, 12

F

face, sand art, 84–87
fishbowls, 34, 93–96
floral settings, 42–56
    centerpiece, 55–56
    flowers under glass, 49–54
    vases, 43–49
flowers, sand art, 49–52
    under glass, 49–52
frames for 3-dimensional sandpainting
    glass and wood, 76–77
    plastic, 69

G

geometric design, 43–46
grass, sand art, 50, 89

H

hanging planters, 38–39
household items, 93–112
    candle holders, 104–5
    fishbowls, 93–96
    lamps, 102–3
    serving pieces, 106–7
    tables, 107–12
    utensil holders, 97–101

I

Indian sandpainting, 57–68
    contemporary, 64–67
    permanent technique, 58–61
    sandpainted objects, 68
    3-dimensional, 69–77
    traditional, 58, 62–63

J

jewelry, 4
jewelry box, 68

L

lamps, 102–3
landscape, sand art, 29–33
layering
    contoured layers, 9
    skinny layers, 20
    straight layers, 8
letters, sand art, 80–83

M

materials, 2–8
    containers, 4–7
    design tools, 2–3
    optional supplies, 8
    sand, 7–8
mirror, 68
mistakes, 15–16
moon, sand art, 73
mountains, sand art
    mountain range, 72
    snow-capped mountains, 29–30
mushroom, sand art, 89–92

N

necklace, 4

O

ocean, sand art, 70

P

paintings. See sandpaintings
Paladin, David Chethlahe, 64–67
pictures. See specific subjects
    choosing, 13
    making, 12–15
planters, 19–41
    cactus pots, 19–28
    care instructions, 41
    hanging, 38–39
    terrariums, 28–37
plastic containers
    construction principles, 107–9
    special problems, 7, 16
problems, 15–17

S

sailboat, sand art, 70–71
sand, 7–8
    choosing, 7
sandpaintings, 57–77
    Indian, 57–68
    3-dimensional, 69–77
scallop design, 19–23
sculptures, 78–89
    decorative cylinders, 78–79
    display cases, 89–92
    representational forms, 84–88
    words and letters, 80–83
sea, sand art, 70
sealing methods, 17–18, 55, 74, 81, 86, 99
seascape, sand art, 69–74
serving pieces, 106–7
shells, sand art, 42, 93–96
sun, sand art, 73
swirl design, 27

T

tables, 107–12
    checkerboard, 109–12
    terrarium, 107–9
terrariums, 28–37
    bottle, 36–37
    cactus, 19–22
    care instructions, 34
tools, 2–3
train, sand art, 97–101
trees, sand art, 98–99

U

utensil holders, 97–101

V

vases, 42–49

W

waste sand, what to do with, 16
waves, 69–70
words, sand art, 80–83